The Passion of Christ

Loving to the End

by
Clare Watkins

All booklets are published thanks to the generous support of the members of the Catholic Truth Society

CATHOLIC TRUTH SOCIETY
PUBLISHERS TO THE HOLY SEE

Contents

1.

Introduction

In picking up this little booklet you are looking at an invitation: an invitation to spend time, and thought, and contemplation before the central mystery of Christian faith - the Passion of Christ. This is an invitation which, at different times in all our lives we will hear in different ways. But for all who seek to come close to the Lord Jesus it is an invitation to which we must, in some way or other respond. And this isn't easy in our own time and place.

In the Catholic tradition we are so familiar with crucifixes and crosses that it seems we can become a little desensitised to the extraordinary power and weakness of the Cross. In particular, we can easily forget that it is, to use St Paul's words, "scandalous", a "stumbling block", and "foolishness" (*1 Cor* 1:17-28, as set out below). It is also, perhaps, strangely embarrassing to us as people of contemporary culture and sensibilities. For the Gospels, however, and for St Paul's proclamation of the Good News of Jesus Christ, the Cross is central, the pivotal sign and icon of the Paschal mystery of Christ's death and resurrection. It is the moment of our salvation.

The hard but life-giving thing we are called to do as Christian disciples is to take up that Cross, and to follow in the path of Jesus. This is a call to the Cross - a call to deepen, in our prayer and ways of living and loving, our witness to the Cross as the place of God's saving love for all people. Christian vocation is in this way cruciform, cross-shaped. To reflect and pray with Christ crucified before us is to ask to be shaped by the cross - a request not to be made lightly!

It is so often the case that, these days, our prayer and thinking is done in a very interior, private, spiritual way; but it seems to me that our tradition of prayer calls us, too, to work with very physical, embodied ways of contemplating God and the mysteries of our faith in Jesus. And so I want to suggest two practical, material things to become a part of however these reflections are used: an image of the cross; and the books of Scripture.

In writing these reflections, and in delivering them to the congregation of Great St Mary's, I have had before me, always, an image of the Cross, and of the Crucified One; and I would like to think that there may be others who not only read these words, and think about them, but also let the words draw them into a new gazing upon whatever image of the cross, or crucifix they have in their homes or churches. These are words that are meant to carry thoughts into new places, and be left behind; they are not meant to be looked at for themselves. They are words meant to be heard in the shadow of the Cross.

They are also words born out of being broken against the Word of God in Scripture. For me the encounter with the call to the Cross was very much through Scripture; and in that encounter it wasn't I who broke the Word, but the Word that broke me. It is astonishing and life-giving to explore more deeply the ways in which the writings of the New Testament witness to the transforming power of the Cross of Christ. I have tried, in what follows, to give a first taste of that witness, drawing not only on the words of Christ from the Cross, as recounted in the various Gospel accounts, but also on the post resurrection proclamation of the Cross, as it appears in Gospels and Epistles. There is a richness there to which we must all keep returning, and against which any thoughts or words of ours need to be thoroughly broken, indeed, smashed to pieces! In the reading of these texts, let there be a good long pause between scripture readings and reflections, to let the words of scripture first speak for themselves. And let the reading take place where the Bible and the Cross overshadow all our thinking and praying, and where we can be enlightened by the power of their shadows.

Indeed, coming before Christ's suffering and death is not easy; but this is where we must come if we would learn more of God's life and love. To go to find the Crucified One is to go to a difficult place: it's horrible, and disturbing and peculiarly lonely. Yet, for the Christian, to come to this place is to visit the heart of the love of God, and the heart, too, of our proclamation of love for and in the world.

This booklet is based on reflections and prayer celebrated at the University Church, Great St Mary's, Cambridge, on Good Friday, 2003.

2.

My God, my God!
Why have you forsaken me?

1 Corinthians 1:17- 28

*C*hrist did not send me to baptise but to proclaim the *gospel, and not with eloquent wisdom, so that the cross of Christ might not be emptied of its power.*

For the message about the cross is foolishness to those who are still perishing, but to us who are being saved it is the power of God. For it is written:

> *'I will destroy the wisdom of the wise,*
> *and the discernment of the discerning I will thwart.'*

Where is the one who is wise? Where is the scribe? Where is the debater of this age? Has not God made foolish the wisdom of this world? For since, in the wisdom of God, the world did not know God through wisdom, God decided, through the foolishness of our proclamation, to save those who believe. For Jews demand signs and Greeks desire wisdom, but we proclaim Christ crucified, a stumbling-block to Jews, and foolishness to Gentiles, but to those who are the called, both Jews and Greeks, Christ - the power and the wisdom of God. For God's foolishness is wiser than human wisdom, and God's weakness is stronger than human strength.

Consider your own call, brothers and sisters: not many of you were wise by human standards, not many were powerful, not many were of noble birth. But God chose what is foolish in the world to shame the wise; God chose what is weak in the world to shame the strong; God chose what was low and despised in the world, things that are not, to reduce to nothing the things that are.

———— ✳ ————

The cry of total abandonment

As I sit before this passage of scripture, looking somewhat distractedly at the cross, I feel myself pulled in different directions. The urgency and power of St Paul's account of his preaching both inspires and shames me: I am reminded of what it is to be a disciple, of my baptismal calling, of the insistent call to proclamation which is so much a part of the Church's work today. And I find myself with questions:

- This being a Christian thing, this call to be Jesus' disciple - how do I find it in my own time and place?
- How is it for me, this witnessing to the Gospel in the relatively comfortable and secure place I find myself?

- And how, from this place, do I look upon this - the Cross, an instrument of gross inhumanity, torture and death - and see in it all truth, all loveliness, all peace?
- How does my life proclaim it? How can it?

These are the questions that St Paul's passionate account of preaching Christ crucified call me to. For what does it mean to us, as Christians here and now, to proclaim this same foolishness that is all wisdom?

This line of questions has unsettled me; for I suspect I, and many of us, have domesticated the Cross of Christ. We have tamed the passion of Christ into a religious symbol, so that we can feel at home with it, or piously moved by it. We have translated the asphyxiation of wracked limbs into the loving embrace of a more appealing kind of divinity. We want the sheer horror of this inescapable truth of what we believe, to be made warmer, more "cuddly", softer on our sensibilities.

I have a crucifix in my hall, but it is deliberately discreet and very tasteful; for what would visitors think if confronted with a realistic image of a naked man dying brutally, abandoned by all? We are pretty much comfortable with the cross as a piece of jewellery, a religious badge, and we have taught our culture and society to be the same. For today the cross is as much an image in contemporary fashion as it is a radical

proclamation of salvation from sin, of God's suffering
and love for men and women. And so, unsurprisingly, our
Good Friday witnessing, our carrying of the cross through
busy towns and cities, full of bank holiday weekend
shoppers, seems unremarkable, or bewildering, rather
than astonishing or powerful.

And we gather in our Churches to worship, to recall
together the story of our being saved, to celebrate
Eucharist together: and, at the centre, is the Cross.

"Lord, by your cross and Resurrection you have set us
free. You are the saviour of the world."

This is our Eucharistic faith; but how can we proclaim
again, in power and truth, this "scandalous" heart of our
faith to a world indifferent to, familiar with, and bored
by the Cross?

———— ❦ ————

Let us look again at the Cross, and remember the words
of Paul which we have just heard:

- We are to proclaim the Gospel, not with cleverness
  and smooth words, but to reveal the power of the
  Cross, which is "the power of God."
- "...we proclaim Christ crucified, a stumbling-block
  [scandal] to the Jews, and foolishness to the
  Gentiles..."
- "...God's foolishness is wiser than human wisdom, and
  God's weakness is stronger than human strength..."

- "...God chose what is weak in the world, things that are not..."

Let us make no mistake: this cross we place in our homes and churches, around our necks, and whose sign we make over our own hearts - this is *scandalous;* this is foolishness and weakness. This goes against all the sensible, reasonable, intelligent things of our own time. To live with the cross as the centre of our living is to put ourselves quite deliberately out of all that the world considers strong, and wise, and substantial, and to choose with God the *"things that are not"*. Have we, as a Church, as baptised disciples, even begun to understand what this might involve?

———— ✣ ————

Today, as at all times, but perhaps more acutely than ever, the Cross reminds us that we are to live "counter-culturally". We are called to live in folly and weakness, in a world that is constantly encouraging us to live in our own strength and cleverness. Like Christians through the ages the proclamation of the cross calls us, in our own place and time, to know *nothing* but Christ, and him crucified.

This, for St Paul, the Apostle to the nations, is the beginning and end of evangelisation: not clever persuasion, or beautiful liturgy, or powerful music, or eloquent argument. For so many of us there is comfort to be gained in being creative and putting on beautiful "performances" and calling it the Church's mission: teachers like me want to give inspiring talks and lectures; musicians and artists rejoice in proclaiming the Gospel in song and beauty; great organisers make events and projects happen, successfully pulling in people, money, numbers. And all this is good, and I for one, wouldn't be without it. But it all runs the terrible risk of domesticating, or "gentrifying" the folly and scandal of the cross, and luring us into thinking this is our project rather than God's.

For Paul there is none of this - only the scandalous, silly conviction that the Christ who met him in power and fullness of resurrected life on the Damascus road was, and is, Christ crucified. Knowing this deep and strange mystery in his heart, nothing could ever matter in quite the same way again. Even what is real, what is, and is not, is radically transformed, turned on its head: "God chose... things that are not, to reduce to nothing the things that are."

How do we bear witness to this power today? How do we build our evangelism, our apostolate, our discipleship on the folly and scandal of the Cross? How, in a culture that is entirely comfortable with the image of the cross on public architecture, in art, and as a fashion accessory, can we proclaim a Gospel in which the Cross of Christ is not emptied of its power?

———— ❧ ————

This is the heart of our reflection. Let us come to the Cross and allow the Crucified One to provide the place of truth and love, in which alone we can begin to respond to such a question. Let us hear His words from the agony of the Cross: "My God, my God! Why have you forsaken me?"

This is the cry of despair. It is a cry of desperate self-abandonment to the God we can no longer feel close to, or comforted by; and it is always present in our world, and, I believe, in many hearts. To be sure, anyone even briefly listening in to the news of all that is going on in our human family can never have this cry far from their hearts: our televisions and newspapers bring us daily images of the shattered bodies of children, men and women devastated by war, and faces contorted with the anguish of loss, despair and pain.

The story of our world comes to us cruciform, if we but recognise it so.

This place of abandonment to a God in whom we can barely believe is a common enough place in our world - indeed, in our own hearts if we are honest. And it is to this place that these words from the cross call us.

To come to this place in all honesty, is to find ourselves without any answers or easy comforts. All we have here is a deep, longing, painful question before God, that terrible "why" born out of all human experience of loss, rejection, suffering. But it is this awe-full "why" that takes us vividly to the Cross, indeed, to the heart of the crucified Christ as he cries out in death. It is the emptiest and most hopeless of questions which, at the same time, reveals to us the heart of our new life, of our being saved. *And we do not do the saving; that has been done for us.*

So how is it, for me, to be a disciple in the here and now? How am I to proclaim, in the Spirit of Paul, that scandal and folly of the Cross for my own time? "What must I do?"

These are the questions we began with - and they are good enough questions. Because we care, because we have some faith, we want to know *how* to be disciples today, *how* to proclaim Christ. But, in coming more deeply into reflection on the Cross that we must proclaim, something has happened to these "how" and "what" questions: they are drowned out by the "Why?" of the crucified one, which leads us into quite another place - *a place of total abandonment to God.*

In coming to the place of total abandonment we must allow our "how" questions, as Christian disciples today, to be taught by the scandal and folly of the Cross. For it is this scandal and silliness that is God's wisdom for our time, as for all time. We must, more and more, take the wise answers we give ourselves as "the debaters of this age", and let them be interrogated by the crucified Christ. And here we will, we can be sure, begin to learn new things - about our selves, about love of others, and about what we are called to do (or not do). It is from this place, and in this spirit of questioning our own wisdom, that the following reflections grow and try to speak of how the Cross is proclaimed in our living.

———— ❧ ————

Let us come to this Cross, this place where the unanswerable question of human pain and hope and life is caught up in the life of Father, Son and Spirit. Let us pray to know, ever more deeply, this power of God's folly and weakness, this stumbling-block or scandal for our time, that we are called to proclaim. And let us pray to meet in the Cross that secret mystery of the power and strength of the Gospel proclamation, which is all to do with Christ's abandonment to suffering in love - and nothing to do with our own skills and busy-ness.

3.

Woman, here is your son...
Here is your mother...

1 Peter 2:21-24

For to this you have been called, because Christ also suffered, for you, leaving you an example, so that you should follow in his steps.

'He committed no sin,
and no deceit was found in his mouth.'

When he was abused, he did not return abuse; when he suffered, he did not threaten; but he entrusted himself to the one who judges justly. He himself bore our sins in his body on the cross, so that, free from sins, we might live for righteousness; by his wounds you have been healed.

——— ❋ ———

The giving up of self

We have begun to think a little about where we are, and what we are called to as Christian disciples. Here we are, thoroughly integrated into our own time, and our own cultures, and it is like this that we come before Christ crucified. We come to a place where our own wisdom and strength are radically challenged and questioned by God's act of taking into his own life the cry of all-help-being-gone, the cry of pain, and suffering, and dying. It is this despair, and loss, and rejection - this *nothing* - that is chosen by God as the way of love and salvation; and it is this that challenges us, we who want *everything*.

Here, in contemplation of the Crucified one, we will try to learn again, and more deeply, of the wisdom and strength of God.

———— ❧ ————

Our reflections so far have suggested that there is something radically strange, counter-cultural, at odds with "the world" as we usually perceive it, in the Christian proclamation of the Cross. The Cross challenges us in some other areas; these areas are three places which I think represent three perceived wisdoms of our own time:

our wisdom about self;
our wisdom about loving;
and our wisdom about being.

These "wisdoms of our time" I want to bring into the bright shadow of the cross, so that we can see them afresh, shaped by the mystery of God's saving love.

Self, loving, and being - three profoundly complex and fundamental aspects of our living, about any of which whole libraries could be (and probably have been) written. Three things, too, about which the cross of Christ has something of its own to speak, in a voice that may be hard for us to hear.

At the heart of the Gospel accounts of Christ's Passion is the *losing of life;* and this dying, this loss of a man's life, is done in public, barbarously, degradingly. Here there is no "dying with dignity", except the dignity of Divine love, which is all but invisible to us. The Cross is a place of death - death with no frills or comforts.

This may seem too obvious to think about; yet I suspect that the reality of this dying is something we generally don't look at. We are happy to move quickly on to Easter as if this made up for it all. But the glory of the resurrection is not meant, I think, to be a "happy ending" to the Passion; rather it speaks of what is truly happening in that real death of Christ on the Cross.

Our reluctance to think about dying - Jesus' or anyone else's - is not surprising. For most of us, however strong our Christian faith, the closeness of death in our own lives - through our own illness, or the illness and dying of those we love - is an appalling and overwhelming thing. We can hardly see the whispers of our own mortality in the failing or pained bodies of ourselves and those we love, without inevitably feeling, some fear, some anxiety, pain, sorrow, and loss. Death is hard for us. It is this hard fact of our humanity which lies at the centre of the story of our new life, of our redemption. Nothing of that fear and anxiety and pain is spared us in the Gospel accounts.

———— ❧ ————

From the Cross itself the suffering, tortured man Jesus speaks to us of this losing of life: "Woman, here is your son... Here is your mother.."

On one level there is here a putting of things in order as Jesus leaves this world: He ensures His Mother is looked after, by entrusting her care to His friend. Those who are consciously facing death do this. But we know ourselves that this leaving of things, this sorting things out so as to be able to go, is desperately painful. It is painful for the dying one, who anticipates their departure in this way; it is painful, too, for those left behind, as they catch a glimpse of how things will have to carry on without the loved one who is to die.

These words of entrusting are also words of departure. As Jesus hands His Mother to His friend, He speaks words which let go of the most significant human loving relationships of His life. The dying man moves right out of the realms of human affection into another place.

———— ❧ ————

In going to this other place, the dying man leaves behind not only friendship, affection, family bonds, but - in some real way - self identity. Again the words of the crucified one simply and painfully direct us to this loss of self. From the Cross the dying Jesus calls out: "I am thirsty."

This ordinary, bodily need of the body on the brink of death has its own heavy pathos; all of us who have been alongside a person in their last days will know of this. Here that same awful sadness is present in Jesus' death. But the request for some small, almost pointless comfort in death is here heard from the lips of the Saviour; in this story it speaks vividly of the particular losing of life which is happening here.

For this is the Lord who cried out to all, "Let anyone who is thirsty come to me!" (*Jn* 8:37), who claimed that anyone who drank of the water he had to give will never be thirsty (*Jn* 4:14). Indeed, this thirsty, wrecked, dying body was described in this same voice as food and drink for eternal life (*Jn* 6:55). Whatever is going on here, in the death of the incarnate God, has seen the fount of all life emptied and reduced to basic, naked need. In His death the Lord witnesses to us in a new way: He witnesses to His being called to a place which seems profoundly to contradict all that He has understood about, and said about, Himself. He is called away even from his own Spirit-filled ministry, simply to commend His spirit into the Father's hands (*Luke* 23:43).

───── ❧ ─────

As Christians we are called to contemplate with great awe and thanksgiving this self-emptying of God for our salvation. Be in no doubt that this divine losing of self in human death is done entirely out of love for us.

But there is more; and perhaps this is even harder for us to hear.

The contemplation of Christ's real death, real loss of self and life on the Cross has implications for our own discipleship. There can be no doubt that scripture, and our Christian tradition, bears witness to this self-emptying as our vocation too. The Cross of Christ is our vocation, as well as our salvation. We are called to share in this mystery of self-abandonment which is the Cross; as the Gospels tell us, we are to take up our own cross, daily, and follow Jesus (*Matt* 10:38, 16:24; *Mk* 8:34; *Lk* 9:23, 14:27).

We are called to lose our lives. It is only in losing our lives that we will find them.

———— ❧ ————

To many Christians this is a familiar enough message; I am not saying anything new here. (That is not, in any case, the job of the theologian.) But the challenge of this seems to me to be a hard thing to bear in our world, our place of living, in particular ways. We are, here and now, part of a culture that sees suffering and death as evils, as problems to be solved, as weaknesses to be prevailed against. When we read, in the spiritual tradition, of the many saints and mystics who prayed to imitate Christ in His sufferings, and when we read the lives of the martyrs, we are very often rather disturbed: is this "healthy"? Is this really what God wants? The voluntary taking on of suffering seems to us symptomatic of some deep disorder which needs to be fixed, put right.

What would it mean in such a culture to recognise suffering and death as vocation in Christ?

My children, I am sure, are growing up in a society where media, education, and popular psychology teach them to prize self-sufficiency. They are encouraged to go out to get what they want; they are taught - quite rightly, in many ways - to value themselves and their needs and desires. And, as their mother, I want them to be happy, healthy, self-fulfilled, and free from suffering. So then, how do I, as a Christian mother, speak to them (and to myself) of losing life in following the Lord? I know that following Jesus will - in some way or other - lead us to Gethsemane, to humiliation, to suffering, and an apparently pointless and premature death; can this be "good news", can it be Gospel, for today? Indeed, in all honesty, how many of us truly desire this for our children?

To proclaim the Cross like this is scandalous indeed.

––––––– ❧ –––––––

Here we are confronted - inescapably, in scripture, in the lives of the saints, and in the Cross itself - by the *losing of life* as Christian vocation. More profoundly, reflection on this loss of life in Jesus' own death painfully reminds us of the reality of this as a *loss of self*. In the end, we, like Jesus, are called even to move away from human affections and bonds, out of our own ministries and works and proclamation, into dying - and called to do this as an act of faith, hope and love. If this is the end of our earthly discipleship, it is an end which shapes all that we do now.

In truth, I'm a little embarrassed by this part of my faith - at least from time to time. Take the reading from 1 Peter we have just heard: it is a beautiful, and familiar passage on the self-emptying in love of Christ on the Cross for us. We can read it and reflect on it and so be brought closer to that great mystery of God's love for us in Christ. We wonder at this.

We are, especially as Catholic Christians, used to becoming familiar with "bits" of scripture - through the lectionary readings, through the pieces of scripture commonly used in the Office, and so forth. We can all too easily miss the context of these passages, and so miss the point of them. This passage is a case in point.

For this reading on the self-emptying of Christ is placed in a longer section, which we would probably find rather less attractive. In this section of the letter slaves are exhorted to obey their masters (even those who are harsh), and wives are told to accept the authority of their husbands and clothe themselves with a quiet spirit. And here I begin to think that, perhaps, we can take scripture a little too seriously, for clearly this can't be meant for me?

Here the cross is used as an example, as a call to cruciform or "cross-shaped" living. It is discomforting. The Cross of Christ here encourages us to self-abnegation and denial of self in ways that, in our own place and time, are deeply questionable, and indeed, for most of us unacceptable.

Surely, we say, the cross can't mean *those things* - not for *us,* in these enlightened times?

———— ❧ ————

Well, I do find the slavery thing very difficult; and remain unconvinced about the submission of wives to husbands. But I do believe that the taking up of the cross as Jesus' disciples, demands some things just as difficult and unfashionable and embarrassing as my being committed to obey my husband; more so, in fact. Cruciform living is not meant to be sensible, or acceptable, or even, in the usual meaning of things, "good for you". Such cross-shaped discipleship is about the loss of self.

So we begin to see how the call to know nothing but Christ and him crucified leads us into a profound questioning of some of the self-evident goods of our time. To live this loss of self as vocation in our own time and place is to shake all our learnt assumptions about what is "good" for us:

- "self-fulfilment", feeling content and happy with ourselves, reaching our potential;
- our working for a comfortable and healthy life, with built-in securities and plans for an equally comfortable future;
- the values of material well-being and success, the aspiring to *having* more and more *things,* the latest, the best;

- the holding of moderate and accommodating views, the refusal of anything that might trouble another, or ourselves, or challenge our comfortable sense of life.

None of these highly sensible, desirable things will we find in the cross. All of them will, I suspect, be found in most of our lives.

———— ❈ ————

Let us be clear, if we really live lives of self-emptying we will be going into some pretty hard places. If we do this we will, each day, take up our cross and follow Christ to Gethsemane, the cross and then to His glory. In this way of following we will be required - little by little - to let go of our lives and *lose* them; we will be sent out to lay our lives down for God's friends (whether or not they are ours!) We can be sure, if we do this, that we, too, will share Christ's sufferings.

Is this frightening? Yes! But may be it is only in so far as we try to do this that we can live truly as Jesus' disciples. As Baptised Christians we are participants, St Paul tells us, in Christ's death and resurrection, and as such we can only be true to our vocation when we are "cross-shaped". This laying down of life, this cruciform way of living, is above all "eucharistic living". In bearing the shape of the Lord's passion in our lives, in losing ourselves, we become, in Christ, truly present to others precisely as "given up" people. We can then be a people of *nothing* but thanksgiving, *nothing* but *eucharist,* in so far as we are people without life-plans, ambitions, personal goals. We become people who long *not,* as is usual, to have their needs fulfilled, but rather to be emptied of those needs in Christ.

———— ❧ ————

What trust such living would take! To trust the Father so much that, in the end, we can let go of the attachments of friends and family, even of our own treasured self-understanding, simply to be closer to Christ in his saving work.

But isn't this precisely what Christ's Cross, whose mark we bear in Baptism and Eucharist, calls us to?

The scandal is that the Cross speaks persistently and clearly of our vocation to be "given-up" people, people learning to put aside our own will, and image, and affections.

To begin to respond to such a radical vocation of sacrifice demands that we return, in poverty and prayer, to the Cross itself.

4.

Father, forgive them...

John 3:14-21

Just as Moses lifted up the serpent in the wilderness, so must the Son of Man be lifted up, that whoever believes in him may have eternal life.

For God so loved the world that he gave his only Son, so that everyone who believes in him may not perish but may have eternal life.

Indeed, God did not send the Son into the world to condemn the world, but in order that the world might be saved through him. Those who believe in him are not condemned; but those who do not believe are condemned already, because they have not believed in the name of the only Son of God. And this is the judgement, that the light has come into the world, and people loved darkness rather than light because their deeds were evil. For all who do evil hate the light and do not come to the light, so that their deeds might not be exposed. But those who do what is true come to the light, so that it may be clearly seen that their deeds have been done in God.

Love as forgiveness

Perhaps one of the hardest clusters of questions in any theological reflection on the cross is that which is concerned with sin. We know, from our tradition, and through the instincts of our faith, that what is going on in the Lord's Passion is somehow about sin. The problem is the "somehow" it is because of sin that Jesus dies on the Cross. And, mysteriously, because He dies in this way, we are saved from sin - whatever we think that means. There is an original and abiding Christian message here, which we can't get away from; it is the heart of our Good News.

But it is difficult for us as people of here-and-now to speak to our own time of sin - itself a language and concept which seems dated, outmoded, unhelpful even. Doesn't the Christian concern with sin, hurt and damage people, when the Gospel should be about affirming? Aren't we running the risk of increasing guilt complexes rather than freeing people to new life? Or so the arguments go. And so we are happier to speak of our weakness, our wounds, and hurt being done to ourselves and others. This seems so much more reasonable and palatable than talking of a terrible, real powerful thing which, at its worst, alienates us from God, and from our very selves. But it is this terrible power, surely, that the Gospel is telling us about. And the difficulty we have with sin is only made worse by the suggestion that the mystery of being freed from this power is to be found alone in losing ourselves to the love of God. This, too, is a hard and scandalous thing to proclaim.

There may be something harder still for us to hear when we think of the mystery of sin and salvation, before the Cross and the Word. This is the hard way in which the cross speaks of *loving*. What is especially difficult here is that, unlike sin, "love" seems a perfectly acceptable, uncontroversial theme for people around us, and for ourselves.

Loving is, after all, something we freely speak of and celebrate in our own time and place, and presents, apparently, no difficulty of language or understanding. This is the problem. For the love proclaimed by the Cross of Christ is, in truth, counter-cultural, and strange to our assumptions about love. And it is, I think, only in hearing this cruciform message of love more clearly and in all its strangeness that we can renew our understanding of the Gospel message about sin, repentance and redemption. For the wisdom of the Cross as regards what love is challenges profoundly the ways in which we find ourselves speaking of and then living "love". *The Cross speaks of what it is to love "to the end."* And it does so in a way which is strange to us - counter-cultural, challenging of our own ways of loving.

Let's consider the common images of love in our culture, the images that fill our senses from films, television, books, art, even advertising. These are the images which shape our cultural assumptions about love, and which, in particular, have a powerful place in forming the understanding of my children, and yours, as they grow and try to understand this troubling place of human affections. What we see in these places are "lovely" things: romantic love, sexual love, family love, friendship love - they are all lovely. They are things that warm us, comfort us, make us feel good about ourselves, things we desire for ourselves - lovely love; exciting love.

We can recall, too, the places we have named love in our own lives: that painful and wonderful energy of "being in love", the wonder of reciprocated love, the joy of the faithful love of friends, the unassailable love of parent for child. These memories will not, for most of us, be without pain; but even the difficulties of real human love carry with them reward, gratification, pleasure, happiness. This is how it should be, as the human experience of love and loving mirrors, in some small way, what we are called to in the love of God. To know ourselves freely loved by another is a really graced and good thing, an almost "sacramental " thing.

Love *is* lovely.

This is how we come here, to the Cross of Christ, and to the Word which breaks us. We are full of our various histories and dreams of loving and being loved, and we come to let ourselves be interrogated by the love of God which finds its saving expression in this - the Cross. Look hard, gaze lengthily upon this Cross, and know what the Gospel tells us of it: "God so loved the world."

———— ❧ ————

This is the ultimate, God-given image of love for us Christians:

- Jesus, betrayed by friends,
- abandoned,
- in terrible physical pain,
- reduced to nothing by suffering,

There is nothing lovely here.

At least, there is nothing in this Passion and Death that reflects the "loveliness" of our happy celebrations and dreams of love. Yet so often we bring our ideals of "lovely love" into prayer, and seek them in Christ crucified. Understandably, in our great, human desire to be loved, we want Christ to embrace us, to put His arms around us; and He may do, and does. But the Cross reminds us of something else, something harder. These arms of Christ ultimately loved us by being *unable* to embrace us, fixed, as they were, to the Cross so as to suffocate, painfully, Love incarnate.

———— ❧ ————

We cannot easily name the mystery that confronts us here. Whatever it is, it calls us to stretch our understanding of loving beyond what is basically happy and lovely and life-giving. To be sure, the Christian message fully rejoices in such fellowship and affection; but we need, from time to time, to look again at Christian love as the hard way of the Cross. This is the cruciform way of loving, which calls us to lay down our lives - and, I suppose, let them be walked all over.

This being "walked over", this laying down of self, reaches, for me, into the scandalous heart of this Cross-centred way of loving. It draws us, in a fresh way, to reconsider sin and forgiveness. For it is *forgiveness,* as the response to real evil, that is the heart of this cross-shaped, selfless loving in Christ.

Here, again, Christ speaks to us from the very place of his suffering and death: "Father, forgive them, for they do not know what they are doing" (*Lk* 23:34).

———— ❦ ————

Perhaps the most scandalous things about this cross centred faith of ours is this consistent, right-up-until-death call and imperative to "forgive". It is, in all human respects, a command to let the one we know to be the offender "off the hook". As such it stands as a permanent challenge to human justice, and our figuring out of things relational.

Can we really let the sinner, the one who hurts us, our children, our loved ones, go free, unpunished?

Yet this is what is happening in Jesus' frequent witness to forgiveness - a witness which he carries through "to the end", to the words from the Cross itself.

This "letting off" which is forgiveness is especially clear when we look at the Greek texts; for here the verb used is *aphiemi,* which means to let go of something. To forgive sin, to be forgiven, is to let go of the mistake, the hurt, the terrible, dark muddles of our living. In this letting go there is a full moving on from, a leaving behind, of the harm done, however real and powerful.

We see this vividly, here, at the moment of crucifixion. Whilst suffering the last, torturous pains of a human body moving violently into death, Jesus prays that this horror done to him should be let go. "Father forgive them..." In these words he turns attention away from who is doing what to who, and why, and how culpable they may or may not be, and lets it all go - "...for they do not know what they are doing". In this profound letting go the Crucified One points our attention to what is, in truth, the reality greater than all sin, and all suffering - the love of the Father.

———— ❧ ————

What we see here is a love which lets go of wrong, on a shockingly deep level; it is a love which, I suppose, really isn't interested in sins. And it is this radically free love that allows the dying Jesus to interrupt the argument between those criminals dying with him. The concern of these thieves, also dying and suffering, is their debate about whether or not they, or anyone else, deserves such punishment. But with this letting-go-love the Lord cuts across their argument and proclaims a new future, in which they too can have a share. This is a future in which the stale old questioning about who did what wrong, and why, and what should be done about it, is let go, left behind. Whatever went on before, Love's message from the Cross is clear: "Truly, I tell you, today you will be with me in Paradise" (*Lk* 23:43).

———— ❧ ————

The lesson of love-as-forgiveness which the cross gives us, helps us hear afresh our own call to forgive. This vocation to love in forgiving is what we pray in the Lord's Prayer, and what we hear repeated throughout Jesus' own life and ministry. It is a message we are called to bear into our own time and place, as his disciples. And it is scandalous - for us today, as for the Lord then.

For how often was the Lord's proclamation of the forgiveness of sins met with horror and outrage from His hearers? And those especially outraged and angered by such foolish loving were the religious and "good" people among them! Unless we know that we are completely dependent ourselves on the radically forgiving love of God (and others) we are likely to find the whole idea appalling, and the practice offensive. The idea is really rather shocking. That, through the power of Jesus' words of God's love to us,

- the sick can leave behind their disability,
- and the sinner can let go the burden of their past, and the entrapment of their present life,

- we can stop fretting about this or that in our lives and loves,
- we can be freed from trying to figure it all out, so as to do better next time,

This is a shocking proclamation, especially for those who work so hard to get it right, and to put it right when it's gone wrong.

———— ❧ ————

We are, for all sorts of good reasons, consistently tempted to figure out the terrible web of sin and hurt through our own thinking, psychologising, and efforts. We tend to think that triumph over sin is something to do with our good religious observance, or our niceness, or the exercise of a disciplined will, when in fact only the living power of the Crucified One, present in His Spirit can cut through this mess and muddle - what the Fathers recognised as the *confusio hominum,* the confusion of humankind. We can, as good, conscientious Christians, treat the living of love and relationship as a kind of craft project, like a tapestry: when we get it wrong, the wrong colour thread, the wrong row of stitches, we must laboriously go back and unpick it, and work it out again. But loving is not "our project", our work of art, in this way.

No. The Gospel message of forgiveness commands and empowers us to let go, in order to get on with the much more important work of loving and living here and now. From this "careless" or prodigal loving we begin to anticipate that blessed and promised future which we are promised from the Cross itself. We are ever called forward to be with the Lord in Paradise. It is that call into the future that can empower us to love-as-letting-go.

———— ❧ ————

Let us see what has happened to sin in all this: it is, indeed, "nailed to the cross" (*Col* 2:14).

The Cross witnesses to a love which has as its characteristic way of expression, forgiveness, the letting go of *all* that has gone wrong. In this light sin takes on a new and hopeful aspect. In the Cross of Christ we behold the place where sin is most radically performed and named; and it is precisely here, in that same place, where forgiveness is begun, and the extraordinary, selfless love of God is proclaimed.

The story of Christ's Passion tells us the one, certain thing about sin that we need to know: that it can be forgiven. Indeed, in Christ it *is* forgiven. However complicated the questions of guilt, and moral freedom, and right and wrong truly are, they are not presented to us in the Gospel, or from the Cross, as problems to be solved. Sin is to be let go, in love, so that the way of God's love can be all the more clearly seen. And this is the way of the Cross.

I sometimes wonder if, in our own time and place, this letting-go-love is actually more scandalous to us than sin itself.

———— ✦ ————

Are we not scandalised, deep down, by such radical, unquestioning forgiveness? To love like this is strange: to say, after the hurt, and the pain, the misunderstandings and the betrayal, the rejections and the denial, and the lies - "let it go!"?

Isn't there something in our psychotherapeutic culture that demands we, instead, figure things out, understand them, put them right, demand justice, or the making of amends? Doesn't this wisdom of the world make for our own well-being, for "healthier relationships"?

———— ✦ ————

If the Cross is at the centre of what Christian love is, then we are called to this radical way of loving-as-letting-go. We are drawn by the Crucified into a way of forgiveness which means letting go on our own "stuff", and that of others. This leads us into ways of loving which are radically at odds with our inclinations.

All this speaks, above all, of an *unselfishness* in loving, which is, indeed, a proper selflessness. It is this which is deeply of God, and only barely echoed in human love. So much of what we call love is based on unspoken contracts of being there for each other, of each being good to the other, in responding to one another, and in ways that we want that response. To be sure, we don't think of our loving relationships in these ways: but from time to time we will be cruelly reminded of this underlying, fallen reality of human love.

To take up the vocation to Christian love which is
proclaimed from the Cross, takes us to a new place. To be
here is to enter into such unselfish love that our own needs
in our loving relationships become as nothing. To go into
this loving way is to say with Christ, as we are betrayed,
lied about, ridiculed, rejected, misunderstood, abused, -
"let it go, don't think badly of them, look ahead instead."
We are being called forward, always, to being with the
Lord, "in Paradise" - together with those who hurt us.

But how can we love like this? What does it mean for us
to be called to witness to such scandal and foolishness in
our own lives? These questions can only drive us again
and again to the Lord in prayer, in whose power alone
this call can be taken up, and this proclamation made.

5.
It is finished

Galatians 2:19-20

Through the law I died to the law, so that I might live to God. I have been crucified with Christ; it is no longer I who live, but it is Christ who lives in me. And the life I live now in the flesh I live by faith in the Son of God, who loved me and gave himself for me.

Living in the passive voice

Every year, on Good Friday, we celebrate the Cross of Christ, His Passion. And it is a celebration. At the centre of this celebration is the most agonising story of a public torture and death, the way to which is filled with broken promises, rejection, abandonment, and appalling loneliness. It is not surprising, then, that the very language we are using here needs some explanation. I have been especially made aware of this in talking to my own children about "Passion Sunday".

For in our own time and place we have translated the language of Passion, and suffering, out of its original sense, into something all together more involving, active, and strenuous. For us to feel something passionately is to be filled with a certain kind of energy. We feel something so strongly, so "passionately", that we must act upon it. We are compelled, by passion, to do something - whether this is in relation to another person, or a conviction, a project, or whatever.

———— ❧ ————

But the Passion we celebrate today is the Passion of the One who is, in the end, rendered entirely passive. The Passion of the Lord, is the Passion of One who appears to us as the victim of others' plans and actions. So, in the end, this redemptive "work" is not so much a task that Jesus takes on; rather something suffered by him, something under-gone. This is, isn't it, a strange and challenging account of how the best gift from God to humanity is given?

God grants salvation, and the fullness of His love to us not through activity, not through signs and wonders, not in strength and majesty, - but in allowing all that is good, and best, and most lovely to suffer and die, as it inevitably must in such a muddled, messed up, world.

God came to us in the power of weakness, and the wisdom of folly. He wouldn't do what we wanted, wouldn't put things right as we had hoped, wouldn't act on our behalf and love us in the way we required of Him. And so we take things into our own hands. It's almost as if the crowds get fed up with all the hanging around, wondering what Jesus is going to do to bring in the Kingdom. They, like us, get bored of waiting on God. Things must come to a head, something has to happen - and they make it: "Crucify him!"

———— ❧ ————

"Something must be done." This cry seems to me so much a part of our lives, as people of here and now, and, perhaps particularly, as Christians today. Life is presented to us, often, as a series of problems that we are to set about solving. We learn and equip ourselves to take control of things - our work, our relationships, our health, our having a family. We make plans. And, unsurprisingly, such is our love of and care for our Church, we do the same here.

We see our Church communities dwindling and aging, we wonder how on earth our children will be able to be Church for the future, we are concerned how to enable young people to discover faith in the Lord, and we fret over how to evangelise in a culture formed by apathy, materialism, and relativism. So, surely, something *must* be done.

———— ❧ ————

I, for one, am glad to be able to think actively into the difficulties and challenges of life; these things should concern us. But before we embark on the next big project, the next pastoral plan, the next programme for evangelisation and renewal, there is something we need to do first. Let us bring our hopes, and plans, and busyness before this - the Cross of Our Lord's Passion, the heart-breaking power of His Word. Let our enthusiastic activity be interrogated by this great work, the work of our redemption. This work was no task, but a suffering in obedience to the Father.

―――――― ❧ ――――――

"It is finished." *Tetelesthai.*

The end of the work of our redemption is given voice, is spoken. And when it is spoken from the Crucified One, it is spoken in the passive tense. This work is not to be seen even as Jesus' achievement, or fulfilment; rather it is a work of the Triune God out of infinite love for humankind. This God who is Trinity, and whose central story with us is the story of the Cross, is in some way quite other from our world. Yet here we see that Father, Son and Spirit, the transcendent One God is more intimately involved with the world of sin and suffering and love than we can ever be ourselves.

It is in the transcendent and here-and-now power of God that the passion - the passive suffering - of the Son becomes, at the same time, the definitive, effective act of God for and on us.

―――――― ❧ ――――――

Tetelesthai "It is finished." Here our own telos, our ultimate end, or goal is spoken of. And this end is spoken of in the passive voice. This is, in some way, to be taken as the answer to that endless human questioning: "what's the point of all this, where will it all end, what is it for, and why?"

Most of the time, most of us, I suspect, answer that question by not really asking it at all. We can - and do - fill our lives up with this or that improvement, or small ambition. There is always the next plan for the house or the garden, the next promotion or job, the next relationship, the next book, the next prayer method. There are countless things we want to do, places to see, books to read, things to try or experience. All this is normal and natural. And these mini-ambitions pertain as much to the seriousness with which we take our faith, as they do the more trivial things of our life. May be if I prayed like this, or read this spiritual book, or tried this devotion, or this spiritual director - then I'd get on a bit better. There's always something new out there I haven't tried before.

——— ❧ ———

But isn't the scandal of the cross - the "it is finished", the passivity of the Passion - a challenge to all this?

Holiness is not, in the light of this witness from the Crucified One, something to be worked towards, a task to be achieved. It cannot be a goal we simply set ourselves. Nor is the bringing of souls to God simply, or fundamentally, a job or project. It is a mystery. It is a mystery born of crucifixion. It is the mystery of God's power which is effected when all our best efforts are brought to this point: the point of crucifixion, of the cry of abandonment, of the losing of life and the letting go of problem solving. It is as our plans, and ambitions, and projects, and hearts are *broken* on the Cross of Christ, that the saving grace of the Trinity consumes all in God's love and mercy.

There have been times - short and horrible - in my own life where the only thing I could do was give up. In saying this I don't mean that I had to give up something, or someone, even. No. It was simply a matter of just radically, hopelessly, "giving up". In particular, I have, once or twice, given up on prayer (though not, altogether, on God). That is to say, I have given up on the task of prayer - on liturgies, devotions, breviaries, and striving.

These are horrible, enforced times, rather than times of choosing. But they are also times, ultimately, of great gracedness and blessing. For in them, as they are endured, it becomes clearer than before what it is that lies at the heart of our call to be with God, our call to holiness. For in this still, broken heart of the matter, we discover the primacy not of effort (although it is often needed), but desire. In our given-up-ness we experience the mysterious hidden growth of Christ's life in us.

And this dawning sense of desire is not our desire for God, so much as his desire for us.

Perhaps this is something we can only really and radically know, when we ourselves have been driven to give up, to put everything down, before the Lord, and say: "Well, I give up. I can't do anything about this any more. You are going to have to." And He does. And it is accomplished.

———— ❧ ————

Perhaps this is where the scandal for the Christian community in our own time and place lies: that we are called to hang on the cross with Christ, to be crucified with Christ, as that reading from St Paul proclaims. Aren't we, in fact, being called, as individuals and as disciples together, to suffer that Passion, to be with Christ in the awful helplessness of the Cross? Aren't we ourselves driven ever closer to crucifixion by a world of doing and fixing things, a world that has less and less of a clue about the power and action of God? Do we dare to "give up"?

———— ❧ ————

"Giving up" things is, in all of its readings, a deeply counter-cultural thing. It is a simple tradition of Lent which leads me to encourage my children to "give up" sweets, or television, or computer games. Yet this simple, domestic, even banal thing is, at its best, a choice against the materialism and consumerism of our time, and a culture which simply rejoices in being able to have, freely and without question.

Deeper still cuts the idea of "giving up" which is the turning away from striving, from trying to do it: this is a dark and risky mystery, close in our own thinking to carelessness, despair, depression. Surely we cannot be called to "give up"? Surely something can be *done, must* be done?

———— ❦ ————

"I have been crucified with Christ; it is no longer I who live, but it is Christ who lives in me."

There is one thing about this Cross which can give us great hope. The Crucified One assures us that our own giving up, our own responding to the call of the Passion to live in the passive voice, will not end in hopelessness, chaos, nothing being achieved. This assurance is based in the faith that it is the power of Father, Son and Spirit which transforms the passion, the passivity of the Cross, into the beginning of new life, resurrected life. Christ is to be known as the One Crucified, the One Suffering, passive. And he is to be worshipped and loved and followed in this because, in all this, *He lives.* Indeed, in Him, is fullness of life. It is the real and living mystery at the heart of our faith that makes it possible for us to "give up" and yet know, in our given-up-living, the extraordinary power of God. In our giving up, our living in the passive voice, we come to know the overwhelming, startling activity of the Holy Spirit, who chooses us precisely in our weakness.

———— ❦ ————

The great scandal of the message of the Cross for us, here and now, is that we may as well give up, if we are seeking to achieve things - even good things - in our own power, by our own strength. Indeed, we are called to "give up in the Lord", to break open our own cleverness and plans, and give the Spirit a chance.

Do we dare? Do we believe enough to hand it over to God? The Spirit, after all, may well have rather different plans for the Church and for the world from our own.

Surely the Cross is calling us to have such courage? This holy passivity, this passion, is part of the scandal we must proclaim. We can only come, again, before the Cross with open, prayerful, even broken, hearts. Here we can hopefully seek to learn - to be formed in - such courageous "giving up".

6.

Jesus gave up a loud cry, and breathed his last

Matthew 27:45-51

From noon on, darkness came over the whole land until three in the afternoon. And about three o'clock Jesus cried out in a loud voice, 'Eli, Eli, lema sabachthani?' that is, 'My God, my God, why have you forsaken me?' When some of the bystanders heard it, they said, 'This man is calling on Elijah.' At once one of them ran and got a sponge, filled it with sour wine, put it on a stick, and gave it to him to drink. But the others said, 'Wait, let us see whether Elijah will come to save him.' Then Jesus cried again in a loud voice and breathed his last. At that moment the curtain of the temple was torn in two, from top to bottom. The earth shook, and the rocks were split.

———— �֎ ————

The cry from the heart of God

In reflecting on the Cross I have tried, for myself first of all, to put all my thinking, and "common sense of things" before the cross of Christ. I have tried to speak about what it might

mean for us to let our own common sense be questioned
there by God's weakness and folly. Now, at the end of these
reflections, I want to let my words be confronted by that great
mystery of the wordless dying of God Incarnate, in pain and
abandonment - the cry of Christ as he gives up his last breath.

In doing all this, I have been forcibly struck by the
challenge that the scriptural account of the Cross presents
to me, as a person of here and now. I have reflected on
ways of being and loving, ways of understanding who I
am, in the light of Christ's Passion which have taken us
to some difficult places.

The Cross has drawn us to *lose* our sense of self, to love
through radical *letting go,* forgiveness, to live not in our
own power, but in passive, passionate obedience to God.

And the truth is this:

- I don't want to live a life of self-abnegation, of
  selfless loving;
- I don't want to let go of my sins, or those of people
  who have hurt me;
- I don't want to give up on the fascinating work of
  mulling all that sin over, picking at wounds, figuring
  it all out;
- I don't want to live only in the power of God, giving
  up my own delightful sense of control, and ability,
  and giftedness.

More than this - I can't. Can any of us?

———— ❀ ————

And yet this is the point to which these reflections bring us: that we, as Christ's disciples, are called to proclaim, and to live these deeply counter-cultural, counter-intuitive things. The heart sinks, as it feels yet more being required of it, more strenuous races to be run, goodness's to be achieved. We are back with the feeling that Christian discipleship is something we have to strive towards. And it is burdensome indeed.

Of course, there is anther option at the end of these reflections. How about we put all this to one side? We can look back at it, and see it simply as an interesting example of what happens when you take things to extremes in religion, when you take scripture too seriously.

Well, we're all free to do exactly that; and, for the most part, in order to make life bearable, so as not to stand out to much, or be too embarrassing, we do do something like that. Perhaps we have no real choice than to fail to live up to this vocation. This is, I suppose, why evangelisation seems so hard for us. Our twenty-first century Christianity is (necessarily?) marked by being normal, by compromising, by not drawing attention to the radical, and so embarrassing, nature of the Cross. But before we go back to such "normality", let's remember something else about the Cross. The Crucified One is, too, the Risen One.

———— ❀ ————

To contemplate the Cross is always to contemplate the crucified Christ, Risen in glory. Indeed, because of the resurrection the crucified Lord is present to us now more deeply, more intimately, more powerfully, than he could ever have been even to his friends in his earthly life and ministry. The reason we stand this instrument of cruelty, torture and death among us as the centre of our prayer, and wonder, and worship is because we know that in it the power of death, and sin, and selfishness, and hopeless striving, is overcome in the mystery of God's love.

Because of this we can bear to hear, and to constantly meditate on these things, and on this calling to counter-culture, and cruciform living. We can bear it - and indeed rejoice in it, - because, in Christ, it has already been accomplished. He invites us to Him. The call is, precisely, an invitation to be with him.

———— ⚜ ————

I've wanted to explore some of the ways in which the Cross stands today (as always) as scandal to our common sense of things. I've suggested, too, that this Cross bears with it a call to us - a call to take up our cross and follow Jesus. The Cross itself suggests this will be no easy thing for us. But it also assures us that - should we find ourselves in our own Gethsemanes, with our own betrayals, denials, abandonment, hopelessness, we cannot fail to find there the Risen Lord. All these things - death, rejection, loss, suffering - He has taken up into His own resurrected life. We shall not walk this way alone, or bereft of his power and love.

For the resurrection is not simply a happy ending to a tragic tale: it is the transformation of that story of suffering and death, through the living and present power of the Trinity.

Our most agonised, wordless cries are here taken up into the eternal life and heart of God; there are no depths - in ourselves, or in the agonies of the world - where we cannot be sure of finding our Risen Crucified Lord.

In this knowledge can we, perhaps, commit ourselves anew - not without trepidation - to living the scandal of the cross in our own time? We cannot begin to respond to this call in our own power; but we need not, and indeed we must not.

But the Cross makes clear - nothing can separate us from the love of God.

"Now to him who by the power at work within us is able to accomplish abundantly far more that we can ask or imagine, to him be glory in the church and in Christ Jesus to all generations, for ever and ever. Amen." (*Eph* 3:20-21.)